Did You

HERTFO

A MISCELLANY

Compiled by Julia Skinner

With particular reference to the work of Tom Doig and Keith Howell

THE FRANCIS FRITH COLLECTION

www.francisfrith.com

First published in the United Kingdom in 2013 by The Francis Frith Collection®

This edition published exclusively for Bradwell Books in 2013
For trade enquiries see: www.bradwellbooks.com or tel: 0800 834 920
ISBN 978-1-84589-739-0

British Library Cataloguing in Publication Data

Did You Know? Hertfordshire - A Miscellany
Compiled by Julia Skinner
With particular reference to the work of Tom Doig and Keith Howell

The Francis Frith Collection
6 Oakley Business Park,
Wylye Road, Dinton,
Wiltshire SP3 5EU
Tel: +44 (0) 1722 716 376
Email: info@francisfrith.co.uk
www.francisfrith.com

Printed and bound in Malaysia
Contains material sourced from responsibly managed forests

Front Cover: **STEVENAGE, HIGH STREET 1903** 49771p
Frontispiece: **HERTFORD, FORE STREET 1922** 71852
Contents: **BISHOP'S STORTFORD, BRIDGE STREET 1922** 71842

The colour-tinting is for illustrative purposes only, and is not intended to be historically accurate

CONTENTS

INTRODUCTION

The county of Hertfordshire encompasses 634 square miles, and incorporates a remarkable variety of landscape. To the north are vistas of rolling downland, and vast modern prairies of cereal crops. Farther east, where the Rivers Lea, Mimram and Stort wind through their courses, the ancient coppices and woodlands have been retained. To the west lie the oak and beech woodlands of the Chilterns, while the southern sector of the county still boasts areas of cattle and sheep pasture amid the increasing swathe of new housing estates and industrial expansion.

In the 16th, 17th and 18th centuries many state officials, wealthy merchants and bankers came live in Hertfordshire. As well as investing their riches in improving and enlarging their properties, a number of them established turnpike trusts to improve the roads; subsequently, many towns benefited from the coaching trade that came along the improved highways through the county. Later, the 18th-century navigational improvement of the Rivers Lea and Stort and the building of the Grand Junction Canal brought the Industrial Revolution to the county. These innovations were followed by the railways in the 19th century, which transformed the county by allowing people to live in Hertfordshire and commute daily into London. Where the railways went, housing developments soon followed. The activities of the house-building arm of the Metropolitan Railway in particular helped bring about the urbanisation of vast tracts of former farmland in the south and west of the county. In the 20th century the growth of motor transport brought about even more radical changes to Hertfordshire, as major road systems were developed through the county.

Among the most momentous changes to Hertfordshire were the foundation of the new Garden Cities – Letchworth in 1903 and Welwyn in the immediate aftermath of the First World War – followed by the designation of Stevenage, Hemel Hempstead and Hatfield as

HARPENDEN, THE VILLAGE POND 1897 39732

'New Towns' following the Second World War. Housing development continues to the present day, as authorities across the county face up to the challenge of meeting the anticipated housing demands of the 21st century.

Some views in the photographs in this book are no longer recognisable, as a result of the enormous changes that have taken place in the county over the last hundred years and more. For example, this restful scene of the village pond in Harpenden's High Street fell victim to the sweeping expansionism and development of the 20th century. The pond was drained and grassed over during the 1920s as the 'highway-valley' village grew into a 'garden-town'. However, despite the enormous changes that have taken place over the last hundred years and more, many people living in the county nowadays, whether in city, town or village, would agree with the writer Charles Lamb (1775-1834), who knew it well from his childhood and described it as 'Hearty, homely, loving Hertfordshire...'

HERTFORDSHIRE DIALECT
WORDS AND PHRASES

'Bever' – a mid morning snack eaten at work.

'Blate' – to moan or complain, also meaning to gossip or prattle on.

'Chaffer' – to bargain, or complain.

'Croons' – cherries, from the Carroon (or Kerroon) variety that Hertfordshire used to be famous for.

'Joskin' – an amusing character, such as a country bumpkin.

'Mizzy mozzy' – dazed, confused, as in **'My head's all of a mizzy mozzy!'**, also used for untidy or messy – **'It was all mizzy mozzy!'**.

'Moggy' – woman, and **'Moggies'** – women, especially when oddly or fancily dressed. Usually a term of mild disparagement, as in **'She's such a flighty moggy!'**.

'Pimmick' – a fool, or silly person.

'Tack' – food, and also used for equipment.

'Then a days' – in those days, in times past.

'Tokened' – betrothed, engaged to be married.

'Wuss', and **'Wusserer'** – worse, and worser.

HAUNTED HERTFORDSHIRE

From Hitchin's High Street a pathway called Aram's Alley runs through to St Mary's churchyard. It is named after Eugene Aram, who was a much-respected teacher at the Hitchin's Church School in 1750. No one suspected he was on the run for a murder he had committed a few years earlier, but eventually justice caught up with him and he was hanged. His ghost is said to haunt the passageway that bears his name.

Bishop's Stortford is famous for its ghostly Grey Lady, who is said to have graced the shops, pubs and alleyways of the town for over 500 years. The main focus of her activity is the shop premises of No 11 Bridge Street opposite the Black Lion (currently occupied by Coopers of Stortford). Over the years, staff working there have reported objects being thrown about, knocking noises, lights switching on and off by themselves, and the sound of feet running down an empty staircase. She is also a regular visitor at the George Inn on North Street, where room number 27 is apparently her favourite haunt, although she has also been seen in the cellar. Staff at the Oxfam shop at 3-5 North Street (next to the George Inn) have also experienced her ghostly activity: objects have been thrown down the staircase, and footsteps heard when no one is present. In the 1970s her presence was also so active at the Boar's Head pub in the High Street that the tenants had the premises exorcised three times.

The tower of the Church of St Andrew and St Mary at Watton-at-Stone is said to be haunted by a grey lady who threw herself from the top when she was spurned in love.

For many years the Bull Inn in the High Street at Whitwell was said to be haunted by a Napoleonic recruiting sergeant – then during building work at the pub in the 1930s, a man's skeleton dressed in the shreds of a military uniform was uncovered. The remains were given a Christian burial and the ghost was never seen again.

Hertfordshire Miscellany

The name of Hertfordshire is first recorded in the Anglo-Saxon Chronicle in 1011. It refers to the area assigned to a fortress constructed at what is now the county town of Hertford in AD913. Hertford's name derives from the Anglo-Saxon words 'heort ford' meaning a place where deer cross a watercourse, particularly referring to harts, which is another name for stags. Consequently a stag features on many county emblems and monuments, including Hertford's war memorial in Parliament Square.

When the Roman Conquest of Britain began in AD43, the Hertfordshire area was the territory of the powerful Catuvellauni tribe, whose Celtic name meant 'battle chieftains', or 'battle leaders' – a well-deserved name, for they are mentioned by the Roman historian Dio Cassius (AD150-235) who implies they led the resistance against the conquest. The extensive earthworks at Devil's Dyke near Wheathampstead are thought to have been their original capital, but the tribal centre later moved to a stronghold known as Verlamion on Prae Hill, overlooking the valley of the River Ver about a mile west of St Albans.

HERTFORD, THE WAR MEMORIAL 1933 85536

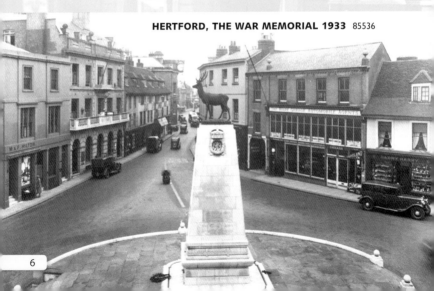

ST ALBANS, THE ROMAN THEATRE AT VERULAMIUM c1959 S2159

Following their conquest of Britain, the Romans built their own town near St Albans, which they called Verulamium. It was one of the major towns of Roman Britain, sited beside the Roman road later called Watling Street, which led from London to Wroxeter in Shropshire. It stood in what is now the area of Verulamium Park in St Albans, and the Verulamium Museum on the edge of the park near St Michael's Church holds a fascinating collection of Roman finds, including a fine mosaic floor. On the western outskirts of St Albans at Bluehouse Hill are the remains of the unique Roman theatre of Verulamium. It was built around AD140 and is the only example of its kind discovered in Britain so far; this was a theatre building with a stage, rather than an amphitheatre. Initially the arena would have been used for events like religious processions, wrestling, gladiator combat, wild beast shows and other entertainment, but over time the stage came into greater use and the auditorium was extended, until by about AD300 the theatre could seat around 2,000 spectators and was used for plays, readings, and, probably, civic meetings.

St Albans is named after St Alban, Britain's first Christian martyr, who lived in the 3rd century in the Roman town of Verulamium that preceded the modern city. After sheltering an itinerant Christian priest in his home he converted to Christianity, but this was a time when Christians were persecuted in the Roman Empire, and he was arrested. After refusing to give up his faith, he was beheaded on a hillside outside the town. A monastic community grew up on the site of his martyrium, giving St Albans both its name and a Benedictine abbey where his remains were housed in a shrine. After the abbey was dissolved by Henry VIII in 1539, its church was purchased by the townspeople to use as their parish church. It became St Albans Cathedral in 1877. St Alban is the patron saint of Hertfordshire, and his diagonal yellow martyr's cross on a blue background features on the county's coat of arms. His yellow cross is also recalled in the yellow background of the shield on the county flag, while the blue and white wavy lines on the flag symbolise Hertfordshire's many rivers.

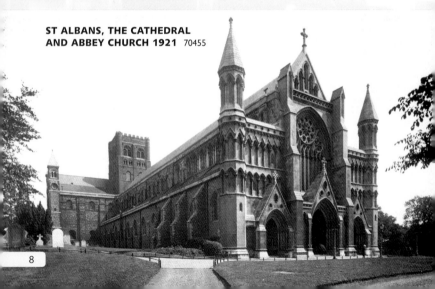

ST ALBANS, THE CATHEDRAL AND ABBEY CHURCH 1921 70455

Easter is when Christians remember the crucifixion of Jesus Christ on Good Friday, then celebrate his resurrection on Easter Sunday. Something eaten all over Britain at Easter is a Hot Cross Bun, a spiced, fruited bun decorated with a cross on the top, usually made of glazed sugar or thin strips of dough, to commemorate Christ's crucifixion. The association of Hot Cross Buns with Easter is said to derive from Hertfordshire, when in 1361 Father Thomas Rockliffe of St Albans Abbey (now St Albans Cathedral) handed out sweet, spiced buns to the poor after the Good Friday Mass, which he had decorated with a cross cut into the top of the dough. Nowadays Hot Cross Buns decorated this way, called 'Albans', are sold in the café at St Albans Cathedral during Holy Week – the week leading up to Easter. The Sunday at the beginning of Holy Week is called Palm Sunday in memory of Christ's entry into Jerusalem before his arrest and trial, when people strewed his path with palm branches to honour him, but it used to be known as Fig Sunday in Hertfordshire, because of the tradition that Christ ate figs that day. It was the custom in many parts of the county, especially in north Hertfordshire, to eat figs on Fig Sunday, perhaps in a boiled suet pudding or stewed and eaten with rice pudding, or with the juice of stewed figs made into fig jelly.

Around 1100, Nicholas Breakspeare was born at Abbots Langley, near Watford. As a youth he attended the monastery school at St Albans but failed to be accepted into holy orders there, so he travelled to France to join the monastery of St Rufus near Avignon, eventually becoming its abbot. His abilities came to the notice of the Pope, Eugenius III, who called him to Rome and made him a Bishop and Cardinal. When Pope Eugenius III died, Nicholas Breakspeare was unanimously elected as the new pontiff in 1154, taking the name Pope Adrian IV. He was the first, and so far the only, English Pope. He is commemorated in a number of placenames in Abbots Langley, such as Pope's Road, Adrian Road and Breakspeare Road.

In 1066 an event took place at Berkhamsted in Hertfordshire which changed the course of English history. After his defeat of the Anglo-Saxon King Harold at the Battle of Hastings in October 1066, Duke William of Normandy marched his army through southern England, pillaging as he went. After crossing the Thames at Wallingford, he reached Berkhamsted. There he was met by a group of prominent Anglo-Saxon earls and churchmen, who swore allegiance to him and offered him the crown of England. William then proceeded to London, and was crowned King William I on Christmas Day 1066.

The centrepiece of medieval Berkhamsted was its castle, but all that now remains of the huge structure, apart from the surrounding earthworks, are the broken ruins of the flint and mortar curtain walls within the bailey. Last occupied in 1469, it once was the residence of Edward, the Black Prince (1330-1376), the eldest son of King Edward III. Inside Berkhamsted's parish church of St Peter in the High Street is a fine memorial brass commemorating an armour-clad John Raven – he was squire to the Black Prince, and he is remembered in the name of Raven's Lane in the town. Amongst the other treasures of the church are two windows commemorating the Hertfordshire poet William Cowper (1731-1800), whose father John was Rector of St Peter's; he was born at Berkhamsted Rectory in 1731 and received his first education in the town. The first memorial to him was the stained glass in the east window of the church, inserted in 1872. All the panels have quotations from his Olney hymns, and one of them shows the poet at his desk with his tame hares. It is now difficult to get access to this window. For the millennium year a new window was installed in the north aisle as a memorial to Cowper, the clear glass etched with quotes from his poetry, images of Berkhamsted and scenes of nature, in which his hares also feature. Two roads in the town, Cowper Road and Gilpin's Ride (recalling his poem 'John Gilpin') also commemorate the poet.

Cherry orchards were once widespread in south-west Hertfordshire, which was famous for the Hertfordshire Black and dark Carroon (or Kerroon) cherry varieties. The village of Frithsden near Berkhamsted is said to be where 'Cherry Bounce' was invented, a liqueur made by steeping cherries and sugar in spirits such as vodka, brandy, rum or whisky for about 4 months.

The highest geographical point in the county is at Pavis Wood in the Chiltern Hills near Hastoe, south of Tring, which reaches 801 feet (244 metres) above sea level.

On the outskirts of Tring is Tring Park, an imposing mansion that was purchased by the Rothschild banking family in 1873. The 2nd Lord Rothschild, Lionel Walter Rothschild, was an enthusiastic collector of birds and animals and established the Zoological Museum in Akeman Street, housing one of the finest collections of stuffed mammals, birds, reptiles and insects in the country; he bequeathed it to London's Natural History Museum in 1937 and it is now called the Natural History Museum at Tring.

TRING, HIGH STREET DECORATED FOR QUEEN VICTORIA'S DIAMOND JUBILEE 1897 T81001

Although probably best known as one of the 'New Towns' that were developed in the decades following the Second World War, Hemel Hempstead has a long history. It originates from a Saxon settlement in what is now the area around St Mary's Church in the Old Town Centre. St Mary's is one of the best preserved Norman churches remaining in the country. Construction of the church begun in 1140 and it was dedicated in 1150, when the chancel and tower were completed. The building of the nave and west door followed; both are fine examples of decorated Norman architecture. In the nave the massive, but beautifully proportioned, arcades have sturdy round pillars with moulded bases and scalloped capitals, again showing expert Norman workmanship. Above the arcades are 12 clerestory windows; 11 of the original Norman windows have survived here. Two other Norman windows are also in existence, one in the chancel and the other in the east wall of the south transept. The church's magnificent spire, covered with fluted lead, was added in the 14th century; it reaches 200 feet (61 metres) to the gilded weathervane and is reputed to be one of the highest church spires in Western Europe.

HEMEL HEMPSTEAD, THE WATER GARDENS c1963 H255043

**HEMEL HEMPSTEAD
ST MARY'S CHURCH
c1955** H255008

From 1290 until 1539 the Manor of Hemel Hempstead was held by the monastery at Ashridge, a community of Bonhommes. The monastery was dissolved by King Henry VIII in 1539 and Hemel Hempstead passed to the Crown. Later that year it received its Charter of Incorporation, which was granted by King Henry to his auditor, John Waterhouse, after he entertained the king with great splendour at his house in the town. Amongst other things, the Charter gave Hemel Hempstead the right to hold a weekly market and enjoy its profits, the seed from which the town's fortunes grew. The Charter Tower in Gadebridge Park is often said to be where King Henry presented the Charter to the town, but in fact, the building is of a later date. John Waterhouse's mansion where the king stayed was demolished in 1555 and his son-in-law, Richard Combe, built a new house on its site, which was itself demolished in 1791. The Charter Tower is all that survives of his house, and was actually its porch. When the New Town of Hemel Hempstead was built, many of its streets were named after people linked with the town's history, some of whom were associated with the Charter of 1539 – hence King Harry Street (after King Henry VIII), Waterhouse Street and Combe Street, after John Waterhouse and Richard Combe.

The Stoneycroft area was part of the New Town development of Hemel Hempstead, and work started in 1952. One of the facilities built there was The Top of the World pub in Warners End Road, which was named after Edmund Hillary and Tenzing Norgay's historic first ascent of Everest in 1953, the highest mountain in the world.

Alongside the River Bulbourne on the south-western edge of Hemel Hempstead is Box Moor Common, which is the final resting place of the highwayman Robert Snook. He was born James Snook in 1761, but his name is commonly quoted as Robert Snook, perhaps due to a corruption of his identity as the 'Robber' Snook. In May 1801, a post boy was making his round to Hemel Hempstead from Tring, when he was held up and robbed of his mailbag by Snook at Box Moor – one letter in the bag contained over £500 in notes, so Snook may have been tipped off. A reward was offered for his capture and eventually he was apprehended in London and brought to trial at Hertford Assizes, where he was sentenced to be hanged on Box Moor on 11th March 1802, as close to the scene of his crime as possible. When Snook was brought from Hertford to Box Moor for his execution, the coach stopped at a local pub for him to have a final drink. Crowds of people were rushing past the pub on their way to see him hang, and Snook

called out to them: 'It's no good hurrying, they can't start the fun till I get there!'. He was hanged from a tree on the moor, and his body was buried nearby. The Box Moor Trustees later provided a white headstone, which can still be seen on Box Moor Common opposite Hemel Hempstead station, past the railway bridge over the A4251 (London Road). Robert Snook has a macabre place in history as the last highwayman in England to be hanged at the scene of his crime.

KINGS LANGLEY, THE VILLAGE POUND c1960 K95053

South of Hemel Hempstead, this strange structure which stands at the bottom of Common Lane at Kings Langley was once the village pound. Overseen by the 'pindar', or pound-keeper, stray animals were impounded there and kept safe until their owners arrived to pay a small fee for their release.

Another landmark of Kings Langley is the magnificent frontage of the former Ovaltine factory in Ovaltine Drive, just off Station Road. The Ovaltine Company came to Kings Langley in 1913 and its main factory there was built in the 1920s, employing around 700 local people to make the malted barley nutritional drink. The company also bought Parsonage Farm at Abbots Langley and Numbers Farm at Kings Langley, and these two properties became 'The Model Poultry and Dairy Farm', which between them produced milk, eggs and barley for the malt used to manufacture Ovaltine. The architecture of the buildings on both farms echoed the rustic 'play farm' built by the French King, Louis XVI, for his Queen, Marie Antoinette, at Versailles.

The attractive farm buildings at the Dairy at Abbots Langley were built in a circular form around a showpiece courtyard; the walls were white with black timber-framing in a Tudor-like design, and the roofing was thatch. The Egg Farm at Kings Langley kept one of the largest flocks of laying poultry – over 50,000 White Leghorns – and is recalled in the name of Egg Farm Lane which runs off Station Road at Kings Langley.

The Ovaltine factory at Kings Langley was closed in the 1970s and the site was redeveloped into housing in 2002, but the factory's listed art deco façade was restored and preserved. The Ovaltine Dairy Farm buildings at Abbots Langley have now been converted into a private residential complex, and the Arts & Crafts-style buildings of the former Ovaltine Egg Farm at Kings Langley have been redeveloped into offices and research rooms for Renewable Energy Systems called Beaufort Court, where the interesting history of the site is featured in the education centre.

KINGS LANGLEY, THE OVALTINE FACTORY c1965 K95056

RICKMANSWORTH, CANAL BOATS ON THE GRAND JUNCTION CANAL 1921 70506

This shows part of the Grand Junction Canal at Rickmansworth in south-west Hertfordshire, which was re-designated the Grand Union Canal in 1929 when it was linked up with seven other canals, and portrays an excellent example of co-operation between barges on the busy canal network. The two central barges have been lashed together in order to bypass those moored alongside the canal bank. The barge horse of one of the craft is being led forward along the towpath and will soon be harnessed up again, whilst the other waits on the right for the manoeuvre to be completed. The bargee of one of the craft stands on the bow ready to cast the towing line ashore, and the bargee woman at the tiller behind him is still wearing a traditional bonnet, even in the 1920s. The photo was taken from the road bridge looking south just below Batchworth Locks. The wooden building on the right is now gone, but the iron bridge in the distance is still there; the small river to the right of the towpath is the River Chess, and the body of water to the far right is now Rickmansworth Aquadrome.

For many years the Grand Union Canal formed the basis of Rickmansworth's economic prosperity, with many trades sited on and around the banks of the canal. Nowadays the town remembers its canal history with the annual Rickmansworth Festival in May. The Festival is organised by the Rickmansworth Waterways Trust and occupies part of the Aquadrome, the towpath between Stockers Lock and Batchworth, and the area round Batchworth Lock. The event celebrates canals, the community and the environment with a wide range of entertainment, but for many people the main attraction is the colourful array of canal boats moored along the towpath – around 100 craft of many types and histories arrive for the festival from all across the country.

The name of The Pennsylvanian pub in Rickmansworth is a reference to William Penn, founder of the province of Pennsylvania in the USA, who lived in Rickmansworth in the 1670s. William Penn was a member of the Society of Friends, popular known as Quakers, a non-conformist sect that was persecuted in the 17th century, and the Rickmansworth and Chorleywood areas had a strong community of Quakers in his day. In 1672 William Penn married his wife Guilelma Springett at what is now King John Farm at Chorleywood, on the corner of Shepherds Lane and Berry Lane, which local Quakers were using as a meeting house. Following their marriage they lived for a few years at a house in Rickmansworth's High Street. William Penn acquired land for his colonies in North America between 1677 and 1681, and many early settlers of Pennsylvania came from Chorleywood, Rickmansworth, and other nearby towns.

Another early settler of the USA was Reverend Samuel Stone, who was born in Fore Street in Hertford in 1602 and emigrated to America in 1633. In 1636 he and his fellow Puritan minister Thomas Hooker founded a settlement at the end of the navigable section of the Connecticut River. They called it Hartford after Samuel's home town, and it is now the state capital of Connecticut. A millennium statue of Samuel Hooker was erected in Hertford in 1999 commemorating the links between Hertford, Hertfordshire and Hartford, Connecticut, which stands on the pavement near the Hertford Theatre at The Wash.

In 1724, Daniel Defoe described Watford as 'very long having but one street.' A few roads have been added to the town since then, but its High Street is still very long and busy. The parade of shops and the Art Deco Odeon cinema seen in this view were built near the pond at the northern end of the High Street in 1929. The Odeon was demolished two years after this photograph was taken to make way for a supermarket, but a building linked with cinematic history that still stands in the town is the Watford Colosseum that adjoins the Town Hall in Rickmansworth Road. The Colosseum was built in 1938 and was originally called the Watford Town Hall Assembly Halls. It has a world-wide reputation as a concert venue renowned for its excellent acoustic qualities; this has led to the soundtracks for many feature films being recorded there, including 'The Sound of Music', 'The Lord of the Rings' trilogy, and the first 'Star Wars' trilogy (now known as Episodes IV, V and VI in the series).

WATFORD, HIGH STREET 1961 W40048

Hertfordshire has a long association with the film industry. Probably the first ever stop-frame animated cartoon film to have been produced in this country was made in 1907 in the studios of Arthur Melbourn-Cooper at his Alpha Kinematograph Works at 14 Alma Road in St Albans. The film was entitled 'Dreams of Toyland', sometimes listed as 'Babes in Toyland', and a copy survives in the Hertfordshire Archives and Local Studies Collection at County Hall in Hertford.

In the early 20th century the pioneers of the British film industry based themselves at Borehamwood because of the better lighting conditions away from London's smoke. Since then a number of film studios have been located in Borehamwood and Elstree, with many famous films as well as television programmes being made there. Elstree Studios in Shenley Road at Borehamwood is home to ITV's 'Who Wants to be a Millionaire?' plus 'Big Brother' for Channel Five, and the famous feature films produced there over the years include 'The Dambusters', 'Ice Cold in Alex', the 'Indiana Jones' and 'Star Wars' trilogies, and, more recently, 'The King's Speech' and 'Jack the Giant Slayer'.

Another famous film studio complex is at Leavesden, north of Watford, which was developed on the former Leavesden Airfield where Halifax bombers and Mosquito aircraft were manufactured during the Second World War. After the war the factory units were used by de Havilland to manufacture aero engines, and then by Rolls Royce to develop a number of aircraft engines from the famous Goblin to the RB211 used on Tristar. The factory closed in the 1990s, but the giant hangers of the former aerodrome are ideal for large-scale film productions and the premises then became Leavesden Film Studios; they are now the Warner Bros. Studios, Leavesden. The series of 'Harry Potter' films was produced there, and visitors can now go on an award-winning studio tour called 'The Making of Harry Potter' that includes sets, props and costumes from the films.

In 1784 the sky above Hertfordshire was the venue of an historic aerial voyage – the first balloon flight over England. The intrepid traveller was Vincenzo Lunardi, Secretary to the Neapolitan ambassador to the Court of St James, who took off in his hydrogen balloon from the Royal Artillery Ground at Moorfields in London soon after 2pm on 15th September 1784. He took his dog and cat with him, but the cat became distressed so Signor Lunardi brought the balloon down to earth for a brief landing at Welham Green, between Potters Bar and Hatfield, where he handed it to a rather startled lady who was passing by; he then took off again and continued with his voyage. A commemorative stone at Welham Green marks his point of landing at what is now called Balloon Corner, at the junction of Parsonage Lane and Huggins Lane, inscribed with the words: 'Near this spot at 3.30 in the afternoon of September 15th 1784, Vincenzo Lunardi, the Italian balloonist, made his first landing whilst on his pioneer flight in the English atmosphere. Having handed out a cat and dog, the partners of his flight from London, he re-ascended and continued north-eastward'. The event is also recalled in the name of Vincenzo Close in Welham Green, off Dellsome Lane. Despite the wording on the Balloon Stone at Welham Green, Signor Lunardi actually kept the dog with him, which accompanied him for the rest of the journey to his final landing point at 4.15pm that afternoon near Standon Green End, just off the A10 road north of Ware. Another Balloon Stone marking that landing place stands in a field at Standon Green End (OS Grid Reference TL3641919792), bearing a long inscription recording the 'wondrous enterprise, successfully achieved by the power of chemistry and the fortitude of man'. And the fate of the cat? Contemporary accounts named the lady who was handed the unhappy feline balloonist by Signor Lunardi as one Mary Butterfield – who then sold the cat to a man riding past on horseback. Hopefully it ended up in a loving home!

Aerial transport of a different sort is recalled at Cuffley, north-east of Potters Bar. In Cuffley's village hall is a model of the German army Schütte-Lanz airship SL-11 that was shot down and crashed in a field behind the Plough Inn on the night of 2nd/3rd September 1916, during the First World War, during an aerial bombardment of London. This was the first German airship to be shot down during the war, and the event was a great morale booster for the country. The pilot who brought it down, Lieutenant W Leefe Robinson of the Royal Flying Corps, flying a BE2 aircraft, was awarded the Victoria Cross and is commemorated at Cuffley with a roadside memorial on East Ridgeway. A few weeks later, on the night of 1st/2ndOctober 1916, a second German airship was shot down which crashed on the estate of Oakmere House at nearby Potters Bar, this time the L-31 Zeppelin. Parts of the Zeppelin are displayed in the museum at Potters Bar in the Wyllyotts Centre in Darkes Lane.

Aircraft manufacture was an important industry in Hatfield in the 20th century, after the de Havilland aircraft factory opened there in 1930. In the 1930s the Hatfield factory produced the de Havilland Dragon Rapide, which was used by commercial airlines all over the world. During the Second World War it produced the remarkable Mosquito fighter bomber, one of the most versatile and durable aircraft of its time despite being built largely of wood, and also developed the Vampire, the third operational jet aircraft in the world. After the war, the de Havilland factory developed the Comet (the world's first passenger carrying jet airliner), the Trident airliner, and an early bizjet, the DH125. The de Havilland Aircraft Company became a division of Hawker Siddely Aviation in 1959 and was absorbed into British Aerospace in 1977, which closed the Hatfield site in 1993. This important part of Hatfield's history is recalled in many placenames in the town, such as Comet Way and Dragon Road, and The de Havilland Aircraft Heritage Centre at nearby London Colney preserves and displays many historic de Havilland aeroplanes.

On the eastern side of Hatfield is Hatfield House, a magnificent example of Jacobean architecture that was built between 1608 and 1612 by Robert Cecil (1563-1612), 1st Earl of Salisbury. An earlier building on the site was the Royal Palace of Hatfield, only part of which still exists, a short distance from the present house, which was the childhood home of two of King Henry VIII's children, Princess Elizabeth and Prince Edward; Elizabeth was also living there in 1558 when her half-sister Queen Mary I died, and is supposed to have been sitting beneath an oak tree in the grounds when she was told of Mary's death and her accession to the throne as Queen Elizabeth I. The oak tree beneath which she sat eventually succumbed to old age, and its remaining remnants were finally removed from the grounds of Hatfield House in 1978. In 1985, Queen Elizabeth II symbolically planted a new oak tree in its place, which retains the connection with both queens in its name of The Queen Elizabeth Oak.

HATFIELD, HATFIELD HOUSE c1960 H254062

WALTHAM CROSS, THE CROSS 1904 51428

Waltham Cross, south of Cheshunt, is the most south-easterly town in
Hertfordshire. It takes its name from the Eleanor Cross which stands
in its centre, one of a series of monuments that King Edward I had
erected in the late 13th century to commemorate his beloved wife,
Eleanor of Castle, who died in 1290 whilst she and the king were at
Harby in Nottinghamshire. Her body was taken from there to London
for burial in Westminster Abbey, and the king had twelve Eleanor
Crosses built at the places along the route where her funeral cortege
rested for the night. Only three of the original crosses remain, one of
which is at Waltham Cross – the other two are at Hardingstone and
Geddington, both in Northamptonshire. The monument at Waltham
Cross has been cleaned and restored several times over the last 200
years, and the three original statues of the queen that stood in its
niches have been replaced with replicas; for some years the original
figures were on display at Cheshunt Public Library, but they are now
in the Victoria & Albert Museum in London.

BROXBOURNE, THE CHURCH AND NEW RIVER c1955 B413049

In the south-eastern corner of the county, the River Lea and the New River form the boundary between Hertfordshire and Essex, north of London. Neither new nor a river, the New River is actually a water supply aqueduct that was constructed between 1610 and 1613 to bring clean water to north London from springs at Chadwell and Amhurst, and it represents one of the most impressive feats of engineering in the county. The New River takes a convoluted route to London from its starting point east of Hertford, following the contours of the land, sometimes via underground culverts, so that there is no sudden drop. A 28-mile long-distance footpath now follows the course of the New River from its starting point to its original end near Islington, keeping to the route of the historic water channel wherever possible, which is waymarked throughout its length with signs displaying the NR Path logo. The Hertfordshire section of the New River Path starts at New Gauge near Hertford then follows a route south past Hoddesdon and parts of Broxbourne before bridging over the M25 near Theobald's Park, south-west of Chesham.

The first-ever railway line to be built in Hertfordshire was the Cheshunt Railway, a horse-drawn monorail that opened in 1825. It ran for three-quarters of a mile from Mr Gibbs' brick pit near the High Street, to the west of Gews Corner, to a wharf on the River Lea. The Cheshunt Railway was an overhead track from which carriages were suspended, which were drawn by a single horse. The original purpose of the railway was to haul bricks from the brick pit to the wharf to be shipped away, but it made history by carrying passengers at its grand opening on 25th June 1825, making it the first passenger-carrying monorail in the world – even if it was only horse-powered!

The first conventional railway through Hertfordshire was the London and Birmingham Railway from Euston, which reached Tring in 1837 through Watford and Berkhamsted, and other lines soon followed. The Railway Age led to the building of another of Hertfordshire's great engineering achievements, the Digswell, or Welwyn, Railway Viaduct that now carries the East Coast Main Line over the River Mimram north of Welwyn Garden City. Styled after a Roman aqueduct, the viaduct took two years to build and was opened in 1850. It is 1,560 feet (475 metres) long and 100 feet (30 metres) high. Its 40 semi-circular arches are built from sixteen million locally made bricks capped with Hexham stone blocks.

DIGSWELL, THE VIADUCT c1960 D223007

RYE HOUSE, THE GATEHOUSE 1904 51417

This photograph shows the front aspect of the 15th-century red brick gatehouse of Rye House at Stanstead Abbotts near Hoddesdon, all that survives of the original Rye House that was built in 1443 and demolished in the early 20th century. The gatehouse, with its red brick and blue diapering, was part of one of the first brick-built houses in the country, and is the best example of early English brickwork in Hertfordshire. Rye House was the setting of the Rye House Plot of 1683 to ambush King Charles II and his brother James, Duke of York as they returned to London from Newmarket; the conspiracy was foiled when the plotters were betrayed, and they were subsequently executed. In 1864 William Henry Teale bought Rye House and its grounds and developed it into a pleasure garden and excursion destination for the ordinary folk of east London. One of the attractions there was the famous Great Bed of Ware (see opposite), which Mr Teale acquired in 1870 and displayed in one of the outbuildings, where couples could be photographed reclining on the enormous mattress.

28

The Great Bed of Ware is an ornately carved and decorated four-poster bed that was probably made around 1590 as a tourist attraction for the White Hart Inn at Ware; the mammoth bed measures 3.38m long and 3.26m wide (10ft wide by 11ft long) and was publicised as big enough to accommodate 12 people at once. Many people broke their journey at Ware in order to sleep in the famous bed, some of whom carved their names or initials into its woodwork. The bed was so famous in Shakespeare's day that it is mentioned in his play 'Twelfth Night', when Sir Toby Belch describes a large piece of paper as 'big enough for the Bed of Ware'. The bed moved around different inns in the town over the years, but was acquired by Mr Teale in 1870 to display in his pleasure gardens at Rye House, where it stayed until the late 1920s when it was sold. In 1931 the Great Bed of Ware was acquired by the Victoria and Albert Museum in London, and is one of the museum's most famous exhibits.

A fascinating feature of Ware that can still be seen in the town is Scott's Grotto, an underground folly built for John Scott, an 18th-century poet who owned Amwell House (now part of Hertford Regional College) from 1768 until his death in 1783. The grotto is the largest in the country, and is made up of a series of interconnecting chambers extending deep into the chalk hillside which are decorated with shells, flint stones and coloured glass. The grotto was restored in 1990 by the Ware Society and is owned by East Hertfordshire District Council. The grotto and its surrounding gardens are open to the public in the afternoons of each Saturday and Bank Holiday Monday between April and September, and the entrance can be found between numbers 28 and 34 Scotts Road, which leads off the A119 to Hertford just past Hertford Regional College. (Note: Visitors to the grotto are advised to wear flat shoes and bring a torch with them, as the floor is uneven and the entire cavern system is unlit.)

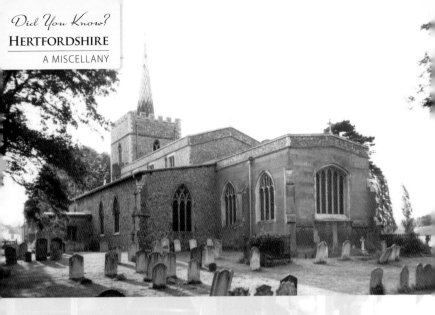

Did You Know?
HERTFORDSHIRE
A MISCELLANY

SAWBRIDGEWORTH, THE CHURCH OF GREAT ST MARY c1965
S67029

A distinguishing feature of many churches in Hertfordshire is a small spirelet, rather like a candle snuffer, that crowns the tower, which is known as a 'Hertfordshire spike'. A good example of one is seen in this view of the church of Great St Mary at Sawbridgeworth, one of the finest parish churches in the county. It appears deceptively modest from the outside, but the interior is huge and impressive. Great St Mary's boasts a large number of memorial brasses and monumental sculptures commemorating local families from the past, which is considered to be one of the finest collections of church monuments in the country. Amongst the graves in the churchyard is that of Joseph Vick, who died in 1888; earlier in life he had served as Corporal Joseph Vick of the 4th Light Dragoons and was one of the few survivors of the famous Charge of the Light Brigade in the Crimean War in 1854.

The first fruit farm in England is believed to have been the famous Rivers Nursery at Sawbridgeworth, which was founded in 1725 by John Rivers and closed in 1985. Many new varieties of fruit were developed there including the Conference pear, which is probably the most popular pear variety in Britain today. It was so named because when it was exhibited at the International Pear Conference in Chiswick in 1885 it was awarded the only first-class certificate of the event, and the judges asked for it to be named in honour of the occasion.

A Hertfordshire spike also tops the tower of the church of St Andrew's Church at Much Hadham, a few miles north-west of Sawbridgeworth. Amongst the other interesting features of this church are the sculpted stone heads, of a king and queen, that are built into the wall on either side of the west door; they are the work of the renowned artist Henry Moore (1898-1986) who lived for many years in the nearby hamlet of Perry Green where The Henry Moore Foundation has now created a sculpture park on his work. (See www.henry-moore.org for information.) Henry Moore also provided the sketch of a blackthorn bush that inspired the Tree of Life window in the west wall, a fine piece of stained glass artwork created by Patrick and John Reyntiens that was dedicated in 1995.

Around 1400, one Richard Whytyndone was lord of the manor of Thorley, south of Bishop's Stortford. This is the very same Dick Whittington of pantomime fame, who in real life was a successful and wealthy cloth mercer who served as Mayor of London four times, in 1397, 1398, 1406 and 1419. Although there is no evidence that he ever actually lived at Thorley, the road that runs off the B1383 from Bishop's Stortford into Thorley was named Whittington Way in his memory when it was constructed in the 1970s.

Bishop's Stortford was originally called 'Estarteford', and gained its 'Bishop's' prefix when the manor of Stortford was awarded to Bishop Maurice of London in 1086. The tall spire of St Michael's Church dominates the town's skyline. Inside the church, the beautiful carved wooden heads beneath the lift-up choir stall seats are thought to be of 15th-century date and to have been rescued from the old St Paul's Cathedral in London before it was destroyed in the Great Fire of London in 1666. The carvings include animals and birds, and some human heads and angel heads.

Sidney Terrace in Bishop's Stortford, which runs off Jervis Road, was constructed in the early 20th century and is said to have been named after the first baby to be born there, the son of a railway worker. Another son of Bishop's Stortford who is perhaps better known was Cecil Rhodes (1853-1902), whose father, Reverend Francis Rhodes, became vicar of Bishop's Stortford in 1849 and continued there for 27 years. Cecil Rhodes is famous for his links with South Africa and what is now Zimbabwe, which was once called Rhodesia after him. He went to Africa in 1870 and became a great adventurer, empire builder and diamond hunter, who founded the De Beers diamond company. He died in South Africa in 1902, leaving a legacy that continues to influence issues of race, politics and society in Britain and Africa to this day. His birthplace in South Road is now part of the Rhodes Art Complex and houses Bishop's Stortford Museum, which as well as focussing on the town's local history also holds a unique collection of artefacts about Cecil Rhodes and the British Empire in Africa.

Probably the most unusual building in Bishop's Stortford is Steps Cottage in Basbow Lane (opposite), which was built to fit the small area of land at the bottom of the hill where Basbow Lane and King Street converge. Triangular in shape and barely 6 feet (1.83 metres) wide at its narrowest point, it is believed to be the narrowest house in Hertfordshire.

**BISHOP'S STORTFORD, BASBOW LANE,
THE NARROWEST HOUSE 2004** B104702

STANDON, THE PUDDINGSTONE AND SCHOOL c1965 S377013

This photograph shows the large piece of Hertfordshire puddingstone that stands near the church at Standon. Puddingstone is very rare, and largely specific to Hertfordshire. It is a naturally-formed conglomerate of well-rounded glacial gravel and flint pebbles in a cement-like matrix, and is called 'puddingstone' because it looks like a Christmas-type pudding studded with dried fruit. It was thought in the past to have magical properties, and pieces of puddingstone were prized as lucky charms or as protection against witchcraft; they were also often given to a bride and groom at their wedding, for good fortune in their union.

It seems that the townsfolk of Buntingford in the past needed only to know the approximate time, for the old Town Clock mounted over a passageway in the High Street has only an hour hand! The people of Buntingford are very proud of their one-handed clock, but to indicate a more accurate time another town clock (this one two-handed) was installed on the pavement outside the Black Bull pub in the High Street to mark the millennium.

Benington is a small village to the east of Stevenage. When the tower of St Peter's Church in Benington was renovated in 1907, some of the carved stone heads that decorate it were renewed. One of them is often said to resemble Josef Stalin, the leader of the Soviet Union from the mid 1920s to 1953, wearing his renowned cap, but it actually represents David Warner, who was the sexton of the church at the time of the restoration work. The story goes that he negotiated a deal with the stonemason doing the work, who was lodging with him. 'Give me a price of a mug of ale,' the mason is said to have told him, 'and I'll put your mug on the tower!'

BUNTINGFORD, HIGH STREET c1955 B245022

On 2nd October 1571, Braughing in east Hertfordshire was the site of the premature funeral of Matthew Wall, a wealthy young farmer. As the pallbearers carried his coffin along Fleece Lane to St Mary's Church, one of them slipped on some wet leaves and they dropped the coffin to the ground – where it fell with such a jolt that it woke up Matthew lying inside, who was not in fact dead, but had been in some sort of deep coma. He frantically rapped on the inside of his coffin, they removed the lid and out he sprang, to the delight of his grieving fiancée. A year later he married his young lady and went on to live to a ripe old age. When he finally died in 1595 he left a legacy, still observed today, to pay for Fleece Lane to be swept clear of leaves each year on the anniversary of his first 'funeral', followed by the ringing of the church bells, first with the tolling of the funeral bell, and then a joyful wedding peal. Both customs are still observed each year on 2nd October, known as Old Man's Day, with local schoolchildren now sweeping the leaves from the lane, followed by a short service beside Matthew's grave.

A less happy tale is told about poor John Gootheridge of Codicote, near Hitchin, whose resting place in St Giles churchyard is marked with a wooden graveboard bearing the curious inscription: 'In memory of John Gootheridge, who died October 30th 1824 in the 19th year of his age. Reburied a week later.' The macabre story behind the inscription is that soon after his first interment there, his body was dug up one night by graverobbers, who planned to sell his remains to an anatomy school, but they were disturbed in the course of their depredation and had to abandon his body and make a fast getaway. Mr Gootheridge's body was discovered the next morning, and he was given a proper re-burial a week later.

STEVENAGE, HIGH STREET 1903 49772x

Someone who was concerned that his body might be taken by body-snatchers after his death was Henry Trigg, who in the 18th century lived in the building at 37 High Street in the Old Town of Stevenage that now houses a branch of the NatWest Bank, seen on the left of this photograph in 1903 when it was The Old Castle Inn. He was so worried his corpse would be taken by graverobbers that he left instructions in his will for his coffin to be placed on a beam in the roof space of the barn behind his house after his death. His wishes were duly followed after he died in 1724, and his sealed coffin was placed on the rafters of the barn. Mr Trigg's bones stayed there in their coffin for nearly 200 years, and his last resting place became a feature of the town. However, poor Henry did eventually fall victim to body snatchers after all – his bones were stolen from the coffin as souvenirs by Antipodean troops billeted in the town in 1917, during the First World War. The barn may not harbour Henry Trigg's remains any more, but this old building behind the NatWest bank still has his coffin in its rafters – surely one of the most bizarre fixtures in a bank's car park anywhere in the country!

STEVENAGE, THE TOWN SQUARE c1960 S191304

In 1946 Stevenage was designated as the site of the first of the New Towns that were developed to ease the housing crisis after the Second World War, and was expanded to embrace an additional 60,000 people. This view shows the Town Square in the centre of the New Town shortly after completion in 1958 – its pedestrianised layout was considered revolutionary at the time. The Clock Tower that forms its centrepiece has become a symbol of the New Town and is now a listed monument. The first pub to be built in the New Town was the Twin Foxes in Rockingham Way. It was named after two notorious characters in Stevenage's history, the twin brothers Ebenezer Fox and Albert Fox, who were born in 1857. They were inveterate poachers but so alike that no one could tell them apart, and their habitual defence when accused of a crime was that it was the other brother who was responsible. The twins were some of the first people in England to be fingerprinted, in 1913, in a desperate attempt on the part of the police to tell one from the other.

One of Stevenage's most distinctive buildings is the Church of St Andrew and St George near the Town Gardens in St George's Way, a striking example of modern church design. It was constructed in the 1960s to serve the New Town and was originally consecrated as St George's, but was re-dedicated to St Andrew and St George in 1984. It is the largest parish church to have been built in England since the Second World War. In the undercroft of the church is Stevenage Museum, where amongst many items of interest is a particularly fine example of a 998cc Black Shadow motorcycle, one of the hand-built high-quality motorcycles that were made at the famous Vincent HRD factory in Stevenage between 1928 and 1955. Probably the most sought-after production motorcycles ever produced, the Vincent machines were expensive but brilliantly engineered. Models such as the Black Prince, Black Knight, Black Shadow and Black Lightning are the stuff of legend in motorcycling circles, and it is significant that out of 12,000 examples produced, more than half survive today. Stevenage Museum has a special display about the Vincent motorbikes, which includes a rare 1936 Rapide bike.

STEVENAGE, ST GEORGE'S CHURCH c1960 S191091

The coat of arms of both North Hertfordshire District Council and Royston Town Council feature a Royston Crow, an old local name for the Hooded Crow (Corvus cornix), which was once common in this part of Hertfordshire, especially around Royston. In the early 1600s King James I (1566-1625) had a hunting lodge-cum-summer palace built at Royston, part of which still stands in Kneesworth Street, a building with two tall chimneys known as the Old Palace. Behind the palace were the royal dog kennels where the hounds were kept, remembered today in the name of Dog Kennel Lane. A feature of Royston is the underground cave by the traffic lights in the town centre, which was discovered in 1742. The walls of this mysterious cavern are covered with medieval relief carvings depicting all sorts of subjects, including St Laurence with his gridiron and St Catherine with her spiked wheel, as well as Richard I, 'the Lionheart', and Henry II. Other images include horses, spirals and naked ladies. No one knows who created the cavern, or what it was used for – it may have been home to a religious hermit, but some people think it was dug out by the Knights Templar for use as an oratory, and that some of the carvings depict their symbols and mystic signs.

Intriguing echoes of the Middle Ages are also found at Ashwell, west of Royston, where medieval graffiti scratched on the stonework of its church survive as messages from the past, in Latin and Early English. Some of the most poignant date from when the terrible outbreak of bubonic plague called the Black Death raged through Europe in the 14th century, in which Ashwell was not spared. One desperate villager left a message that has been translated as: '1350 – miserable wild distracted the dregs of the people alone survive to witness and tell the tale.' A less tragic message records the disgust of a stonemason with a colleague's poor workmanship: 'The corners are not jointed correctly – I spit on them.' Other graffiti include: 'The Archdeacon is an ass', 'Drunkenness breaks whatever wisdom touches', and 'Barbara is a regular young vixen'.

HITCHIN, SUN STREET 1901 46635

Sun Street in Hitchin is named after the Sun Hotel, one of the town's most important coaching inns in the past. In 1722, three highwaymen held up the landlord and the inn's guests at gunpoint, robbed them and tied them up before making off with their plunder; as they left the inn, the highwaymen scratched their initials, and the date, into the bricks above the door arch, where they can still be seen.

Hitchin is home to the unique British Schools Museum, housed in the former Hitchin British School buildings in Queen Street. The museum holds the country's best collection of objects relating to the history of elementary education from pre-Victorian times to the late 1960s, including the only complete schoolroom left in Britain based on the Lancasterian, or 'Monitorial', system of education developed by Joseph Lancaster; this relied upon older children, called monitors, to teach and supervise younger pupils, allowing large numbers of children to be supervised by a single teacher. School parties regularly visit the museum, where their pupils can experience a taste of education methods in the past.

WELWYN GARDEN CITY, PARKWAY, THE FOUNTAIN c1960 W294080

In the late 1890s Ebenezer Howard developed the concept of Garden Cities, 'model' low density communities in which industry and dwellings would be segregated and ample open space planned, combining the best of town and country living. His two pioneer ventures were both in Hertfordshire. Letchworth was Britain's first 'Garden City', planned in 1903, and Welwyn Garden City followed later, founded in 1920. A feature of Welwyn Garden City is Parkway, a central mall, almost a mile long, that forms the spine of the town and epitomises the green open spaces in which Ebenezer Howard delighted; this fountain on Parkway stands as a memorial to his foresight. Welwyn Garden City was also designated a New Town in 1948, and is thus unique in Britain in being both a Garden City and a New Town, exemplifying the physical, social and cultural planning ideals of the periods in which it was planned and developed.

Evidence of much earlier settlement in the Welwyn area can be found beneath Junction 6 of the A1(M) motorway, where the remains of a Roman bath house are ingeniously preserved in a steel vault, all that remains of a luxurious Roman villa that once stood here. The Welwyn Roman Baths are open to the public, with an exhibition about the history of the site and displays of archaeological finds from the area.

One of the early buildings at Letchworth was this fantastic structure in Barrington Road called The Cloisters, designed by William Harrison Cowlishaw, a British architect of the Arts and Crafts school. This quirky building was constructed in 1906-7 for Miss Annie Jane Lawrence as a theosophical meditation centre and open-air school, where students were encouraged to study 'how thought affects action and what causes and produces thought' whilst developing healthy minds through outdoor living. The design of the building made startlingly original use of traditional materials and familiar decoration, but engendered a mixed reaction from critics. However, it is now a Grade 2* listed building and has been designated as one of the 'great historic buildings of North Hertfordshire'.

LETCHWORTH, THE CLOISTERS 1908 60889

As well as being the first Garden City, Letchworth is also the site of the first roundabout on a public road in the United Kingdom, 'Sollershott Circus', which was built in 1909 as part of the original layout of the Garden City. It is located at the junction of Broadway, Spring Road and Sollershott East and West, a short distance from Broadway Gardens, and marked with two signs proclaiming its place in highway history. However, when it was first built, traffic could circulate around the central island in both directions, the usual roundabout flow system not being adopted until the 1920s, so it was probably as baffling to motorists then as the Plough Roundabout at Hemel Hempstead is to the drivers of today, named after the now demolished Plough public house that used to stand on the site. It consists of a circular road with traffic moving in both directions, with a series of mini-roundabouts to negotiate at each junction, each of which have two lanes around them. It is known locally as 'The Magic Roundabout' and is one of Hemel Hempstead's more notorious claims to fame.

HEMEL HEMPSTEAD, THE MAGIC ROUNDABOUT 2005 H255717

Highway history of a different sort is recalled in the story of Lady Katherine Ferrers, a notorious character in Hertfordshire's story. Just off the A5 at Markyate, a few miles north-west of Harpenden, is an impressive Jacobean house that is now called Cell Park but was previously known as Markyate Cell. In the 17th century Lady Katherine lived there with her husband, Sir Thomas Fanshawe. Born in 1634, Katherine had married Thomas when she was 14, but grew into a wild and spirited young woman who became bored with her husband and the dull way they lived. To amuse herself she lived a secret life at night as a 'highwayman', dressed as a man in breeches, cloak, mask and tricorn hat which she kept in a secret room hidden behind the fireplace of her bedchamber in the eastern wing of the house. There she would change into her garb before leaving the house by a secret staircase to ride out on her horse in search of travellers to hold up at gunpoint and rob of their valuables. Her first victim was her sister-in-law, who she disliked intensely, who she held up and robbed one night after the lady had come to dinner at Markyate Cell and was on her way home – and Sir Thomas put up a reward to capture the highwayman, never guessing that the villain was actually his own wife!

Katherine led her double life for several years, as an elegant lady by day and an audacious 'lady of of the road' terrorising travellers by night, until in 1660 she was shot by one of her victims during a hold-up on Nomansland Common, near Harpenden. She managed to get back home to Markyate Cell before she collapsed and died. The next morning her body was found lying at the foot of the east wall of the house, near the hidden staircase leading up to her secret room, and the shocked Fanshawes realised what she had been up to all this time. Lady Katherine's story was made famous in the classic feature film 'The Wicked Lady' of 1945, starring Margaret Lockwood.

SPORTING HERTFORDSHIRE

Samuel Ryder came to live in St Albans in 1895, where he made his fortune selling penny packets of plant seeds. After convalescing from an illness in 1908, he took up playing golf to get more fresh air for the good of his health. He became enthusiastic about the game and joined Verulam Golf Club at St Albans, where he served as Captain of the Club in 1911, 1926 and 1927. He became involved supporting professional golfing events, and in 1926 he donated the gold Ryder Cup trophy for a biennial competition between the best professional golfers in the United States and the United Kingdom; the first official Ryder Cup competition took place in 1927, and since then it has developed into golf's most important team competition. The Verulam Golf Club now proudly proclaims itself 'the home of the Ryder Cup'.

Another famous name from Hertfordshire in golfing history is Sir Nick Faldo, one of the top players of his era, who was born in Welwyn Garden City in 1975 and played his early golf at Welwyn Garden City Golf Club. Faldo has won more major golf championships than any European player since 1914, and is also the most successful Ryder Cup player ever – he has won the most points of any player on either team (25) and also holds the record for having played the most Ryder Cup matches.

Some histories of Hertfordshire record cricket being played on the Common at Redbourn in 1666 – making Redbourn one of the oldest recorded cricketing locations in England, and also the first place in the county where the game is known to have been played. The Redbourn Cricket Club of today was formed around 1823 and won the County Challenge Cup for three consecutive years in the 19th century, in 1888, 1889 and 1890; this achievement won the club the right to keep the silver trophy, which is still a proud possession of the club.

Not many towns can claim a British Formula One World Champion racing driver amongst their famous sons – but Stevenage can. Lewis Hamilton, MBE, was born there in 1985. He began his driving career in 1993, at the age of 8, karting at the Rye House Kart Circuit near Hoddesdon.

Bishop's Stortford Football Club won the FA Amateur Cup in the 1973-74 season. The 1980-81 season was also memorable when Stortford won the FA Trophy with a 1-0 victory over Sutton United at Wembley – becoming the first ever football club to have captured both trophies.

When Stevenage Football Club won the FA Trophy in 2007, beating Kidderminster Harriers 3–2, it was the first competitive club game and cup final to be held at the new Wembley Stadium.

Watford Football Club was founded in 1881 as Watford Rovers, and the club was renamed West Hertfordshire after becoming the football section of West Hertfordshire Sports Club in 1890. West Hertfordshire then merged with local rivals Watford St Mary's in 1898, and the merged team was named Watford Football Club, which moved to its present home at Vicarage Road in 1922. Watford FC is famous for its association with the pop star and lifelong Watford supporter Sir Elton John, who was Chairman of Watford FC from 1976 until 1987, and again from 1997 until 2002. Sir Elton also appointed the club's most successful manager in Graham Taylor, who took the club from the Fourth Division to the First Division and led Watford to the FA Cup Final in 1984 (they lost 2-0 to Everton). Sir Elton John now serves with Graham Taylor as joint Honorary Life President of the club. At home matches, Watford FC's supporters traditionally enter the stadium to the theme tune of 'Z Cars', a popular TV police drama of the 1960s and 70s. This custom dates back to the 1963-64 season when Bill McGarry managed Watford, and 'Z Cars' was his favourite TV programme.

QUIZ QUESTIONS

Answers on page 52.

1. What is the traditional nickname for a person born and bred in Hertfordshire?

2. North-west of Welwyn Garden City is Ayot St Lawrence, where the writer and playwright George Bernard Shaw came to live in 1906, and where he wrote 'Pygmalion', 'Back to Methuselah' and 'Saint Joan'. His former home, Shaw's Corner, is now open to the public as a National Trust property. What reason did George Bernard Shaw give for his decision to move to Ayot St Lawrence?

3. What sport is played by the Watford Cheetahs?

4. 'The heart of a town lies in its people' is the motto of which Hertfordshire town?

5. Which Hertfordshire village has a particularly fine type of sausage named after it?

6. Hertford is believed to appear disguised as 'Meryton' in which famous novel?

7. One of the beers produced by the Tring Brewery is called 'Jack o' Legs'. It is named after a popular figure in Hertfordshire folklore from medieval times, a Robin-Hood style character who stole from the rich and gave to the poor before he was caught and executed. However, he did not live in Tring – which Hertfordshire village is particularly associated with him?

8. Where in Hertfordshire can you find a building known locally as 'Castle Corset'?

9. A relic of crime and punishment in former times can be found on the village green at Datchworth, south-east of Stevenage. What is it?

10. A famous landmark of St Albans is the Clock Tower in the centre of the city, which is the only medieval clock tower in the country. It is open to the public at weekends and bank holidays, and climbing the 93 steps up the spiral staircase inside it takes the visitor through the five internal stories to the roof, where there is a wonderful view of the city and St Albans Cathedral. The tower was built in the early 15th century to house the great bell Gabriel, which was named for the Archangel Gabriel and cast with a Latin inscription around it that translates as 'From Heaven I come/ Gabriel my name'. Gabriel sounded in the evening to announce the curfew, when all fires must be doused in the houses of the timber-framed town, and in the morning to rouse apprentices to their work. It also rang to raise the alarm in the event of fires or affray, as when the town came under surprise attack in the first battle of St Albans, one of two battles that were fought in and around the town – in which conflict?

ST ALBANS, THE CLOCK TOWER AND MARKET CROSS 1921 70477

RECIPE

WATERCRESS SOUP

Watercress was an important crop in Hertfordshire in the past, particularly from the watercress beds of the Rivers Gade and Bulbourne around Hemel Hempstead and Berkhamsted. A last vestige of Hertfordshire's watercress industry remains at Whitwell, near Hitchin, at the Nine Wells Watercress Farm. Watercress has a distinctive peppery flavour, and makes a delicious soup. Serves 4-6.

> 2-3 bunches or bags of watercress
>   (approximately 200g/7oz total weight)
> 25g/1oz butter
> 1 medium sized onion, peeled and chopped
> 225g/8oz potatoes, peeled and chopped
> 1.2 litres/2 pints chicken or vegetable stock
> Salt and freshly ground black pepper
> Freshly grated nutmeg, to serve (optional)
> 125ml/4 fl oz single cream, crème fraîche or
>   natural yogurt, to serve (optional)

Melt the butter in a large saucepan and cook the onion over a medium heat for 4-5 minutes, until soft and transparent but not browned. Add the potatoes and cook for a further 4-5 minutes, then add the stock. Chop through the bunches of watercress about one third from the leafy ends, and retain the leafy section for later. Roughly chop the stalks and any remaining leaves, and add to the pan – the stalks help flavour the soup. Bring to the boil, then reduce the heat, cover the pan and simmer gently for about 20 minutes, until the potato pieces are soft and tender. Stir in the reserved watercress and allow to heat through for about 3 minutes. Remove the pan from the heat and allow the soup to cool for a few minutes, then liquidise with a blender or food processor. Return the soup to the pan, reheat and season to taste with salt and freshly ground black pepper, and a little freshly grated nutmeg, if using. Add a swirl of single cream, crème fraîche or natural yogurt to each helping if liked.

RECIPE

PUCKERIDGE FARM BREAD

This easy recipe for a fruited tea bread comes from Puckeridge, a village in east Hertfordshire between Bishop's Stortford and Stevenage. When making this, remember to soak the sultanas in (milkless) tea in good time before you need them – this makes the fruit lovely and soft, resulting in a deliciously moist and tasty tea bread.

> 175g/6oz sultanas
> 250ml/9fl oz hot milkless tea
> 115g/4oz demerara sugar
> 225g/8oz self-raising flour
>   (either white or brown self-raising flour works well)
> 1 egg, beaten

Place the sultanas in a bowl, add the hot, milkless tea, cover the bowl and leave to soak for at least 5 hours, preferably overnight.

Pre-heat the oven to 180°C/350°F/Gas Mark 4 (slightly less for a fan oven). Grease a 900g/2lb loaf tin.

Put the flour and sugar into a large mixing bowl. Stir in the sultanas and the remaining soaking liquid, and then the beaten egg. Mix it all together well, then pour the mixture into the loaf tin. Bake just below the centre of the pre-heated oven for about 45 minutes, until it is well risen and golden, and firm to the touch – check the cake towards the end of the cooking time, and bake for a little longer if it looks like it can take it. Leave to settle in the tin for 15 minutes before turning out onto a wire tray to cool.

This can be eaten warm or cold, cut into slices and spread with butter.

QUIZ ANSWERS

1. A Hertfordshire Hedgehog.

2. George Bernard Shaw said that he chose Ayot St Lawrence as his home when he noticed a tombstone in the local churchyard which reads: 'Mary Ann South, born 1825, died 1895. Her time was short' – if the local people thought a life of 70 years was short, he was sure that was the place for him! Indeed, GBS lived there until he died in 1950, at the grand old age of 94.

3. The Watford Cheetahs are an American Football team who play their home games at Fullerians Rugby Football Club.

4. Stevenage.

5. The Braughing Sausage is named after the village of Braughing in east Hertfordshire, where the recipe was devised by a local butcher, Douglas White, in 1954, and sold from his shop at 15 Green End. It proved so popular that it soon became one of Hertfordshire's food legends. Braughing Sausages continue to be made to Douglas White's exact recipe, and are still sold from the original D White's Butchers shop at Braughing; they are also available online from www.braughingsausage.com.

6. Jane Austen's famous novel 'Pride and Prejudice' is set mainly in Hertfordshire, and she is thought to have fictionalised Hertford as 'Meryton' in the book. If this is so, then the ball where Elizabeth Bennet met Mr Darcy for the first time would have been held at the Assembly Rooms in Hertford's Shire Hall, the prominent building with a clock in the centre distance of the photograph on the title page of this book.

7. The legend of Jack o' Legs is associated with Weston, south of Baldock, where a sign on the village green tells his story. Jack earned his nickname because he was an exceptionally tall man, and the purported site of his final resting place can be seen in the local churchyard, where a wooden sign board stands between two stones 14 feet (4.3 metres) apart that are supposed to mark the head and foot of his grave.

8. A significant building in Letchworth from its early days is the former Spirella Corset Factory in Bridge Road, affectionately known locally as 'Castle Corset'. The factory was designed by Cecil Hignett and built between 1912-20, fulfilling Ebenezer Howard's tenet that his new Garden City should provide industrial employment and not merely be a dormitory town for London. With its reinforced concrete and glass structure disguised by brick facings and gabled pavilions, the building resembles an updated version of the Arts & Crafts style of architecture. The corset factory was Letchworth's biggest employer for almost eighty years, and the Spirella Building remains a much-loved Letchworth landmark in its present role as a multi-tenanted business centre.

9. A whipping post. A plaque on the post records that it was last used in 1665, when 'two vagabonds were publicly flogged here'.

10. Both battles of St Albans took place during the Wars of the Roses of the 15th century, fought between two rival royal factions claiming the throne, the Houses of Lancaster and York. The first battle of St Albans was fought on 22nd May 1455 when the Yorkists launched a surprise attack on the town; after the battle, the victorious Yorkist troops set about plundering the town. The second battle of St Albans, on 17th February 1461, saw a victory for the Lancastrians.

FRANCIS FRITH

PIONEER   VICTORIAN   PHOTOGRAPHER

Francis Frith, founder of the world-famous photographic archive, was a complex and multi-talented man. A devout Quaker and a highly successful Victorian businessman, he was philosophical by nature and pioneering in outlook. By 1855 he had already established a wholesale grocery business in Liverpool, and sold it for the astonishing sum of £200,000, which is the equivalent today of over £15,000,000. Now in his thirties, and captivated by the new science of photography, Frith set out on a series of pioneering journeys up the Nile and to the Near East.

INTRIGUE AND EXPLORATION

He was the first photographer to venture beyond the sixth cataract of the Nile. Africa was still the mysterious 'Dark Continent', and Stanley and Livingstone's historic meeting was a decade into the future. The conditions for picture taking confound belief. He laboured for hours in his wicker dark-room in the sweltering heat of the desert, while the volatile chemicals fizzed dangerously in their trays. Back in London he exhibited his photographs and was 'rapturously cheered' by members of the Royal Society. His reputation as a photographer was made overnight.

VENTURE OF A LIFE-TIME

By the 1870s the railways had threaded their way across the country, and Bank Holidays and half-day Saturdays had been made obligatory by Act of Parliament. All of a sudden the working man and his family were able to enjoy days out, take holidays, and see a little more of the world.

With typical business acumen, Francis Frith foresaw that these new tourists would enjoy having souvenirs to commemorate their days out. For the next thirty years he travelled the country by train and by pony and trap, producing fine photographs of seaside resorts and beauty spots that were keenly bought by millions of Victorians. These prints were painstakingly pasted into family albums and pored over during the dark nights of winter, rekindling precious memories of summer excursions. Frith's studio was soon supplying retail shops all over the country, and by 1890 F Frith & Co had become the greatest specialist photographic publishing company in the world, with over 2,000 sales outlets, and pioneered the picture postcard.

FRANCIS FRITH'S LEGACY

Francis Frith had died in 1898 at his villa in Cannes, his great project still growing. By 1970 the archive he created contained over a third of a million pictures showing 7,000 British towns and villages.

Frith's legacy to us today is of immense significance and value, for the magnificent archive of evocative photographs he created provides a unique record of change in the cities, towns and villages throughout Britain over a century and more. Frith and his fellow studio photographers revisited locations many times down the years to update their views, compiling for us an enthralling and colourful pageant of British life and character.

We are fortunate that Frith was dedicated to recording the minutiae of everyday life. For it is this sheer wealth of visual data, the painstaking chronicle of changes in dress, transport, street layouts, buildings, housing and landscape that captivates us so much today, offering us a powerful link with the past and with the lives of our ancestors.

Computers have now made it possible for Frith's many thousands of images to be accessed almost instantly. The archive offers every one of us an opportunity to examine the places where we and our families have lived and worked down the years. Its images, depicting our shared past, are now bringing pleasure and enlightenment to millions around the world a century and more after his death.

For further information visit: www.francisfrith.com

INTERIOR DECORATION

Frith's photographs can be seen framed and as giant wall murals in thousands of pubs, restaurants, hotels, banks, retail stores and other public buildings throughout Britain. These provide interesting and attractive décor, generating strong local interest and acting as a powerful reminder of gentler days in our increasingly busy and frenetic world.

FRITH PRODUCTS

All Frith photographs are available as prints and posters in a variety of different sizes and styles. In the UK we also offer a range of other gift and stationery products illustrated with Frith photographs, although many of these are not available for delivery outside the UK – see our web site for more information on the products available for delivery in your country.

THE INTERNET

Over 100,000 photographs of Britain can be viewed and purchased on the Frith web site. The web site also includes memories and reminiscences contributed by our customers, who have personal knowledge of localities and of the people and properties depicted in Frith photographs. If you wish to learn more about a specific town or village you may find these reminiscences fascinating to browse. Why not add your own comments if you think they would be of interest to others? See **www.francisfrith.com**

PLEASE HELP US BRING FRITH'S PHOTOGRAPHS TO LIFE

Our authors do their best to recount the history of the places they write about. They give insights into how particular towns and villages developed, they describe the architecture of streets and buildings, and they discuss the lives of famous people who lived there. But however knowledgeable our authors are, the story they tell is necessarily incomplete.

Frith's photographs are so much more than plain historical documents. They are living proofs of the flow of human life down the generations. They show real people at real moments in history; and each of those people is the son or daughter of someone, the brother or sister, aunt or uncle, grandfather or grandmother of someone else. All of them lived, worked and played in the streets depicted in Frith's photographs.

We would be grateful if you would give us your insights into the places shown in our photographs: the streets and buildings, the shops, businesses and industries. Post your memories of life in those streets on the Frith website: what it was like growing up there, who ran the local shop and what shopping was like years ago; if your workplace is shown tell us about your working day and what the building is used for now. Read other visitors' memories and reconnect with your shared local history and heritage. With your help more and more Frith photographs can be brought to life, and vital memories preserved for posterity, and for the benefit of historians in the future.

Wherever possible, we will try to include some of your comments in future editions of our books. Moreover, if you spot errors in dates, titles or other facts, please let us know, because our archive records are not always completely accurate—they rely on 140 years of human endeavour and hand-compiled records. You can email us using the contact form on the website.

Thank you!

For further information, trade, or author enquiries
please contact us at the address below:

**The Francis Frith Collection, 6 Oakley Business Park,
Wylye Road, Dinton, Wiltshire SP3 5EU.**
Tel: +44 (0)1722 716 376 Fax: +44 (0)1722 716 881
e-mail: sales@francisfrith.co.uk **www.francisfrith.com**